Managing the Careers of Professional Knowledge Workers

Juani Swart

Nicholas Kinnie

Work and Employment Research Centre,

School of Management, University of Bath

First published 2004

Cover design by Curve
Designed and typeset by Beacon GDT
Printed in Great Britain by Short Run Press

British Library Cataloguing in Publication Data
A catalogue record for this book is available from the British Library

ISBN 1 84398 065 7

Chartered Institute of Personnel and Development,
CIPD House, Camp Road, London SW19 4UX

Tel: 020 8971 9000
Fax: 020 8263 3333
Website: www.cipd.co.uk

Incorporated by Royal Charter. Registered charity no. 1079797.

Contents

List of figures and tables

Acknowledgements

We would like to extend our sincere thanks to the CIPD for funding the research on the links between people management and performance in knowledge-intensive firms. In particular, we would like to thank Angela Baron for her continued support and patience during the research and writing phases.

We would also like to thank the participating organisations who made this research possible.

Finally, much of the analysis could not have been done without the support of the wider WERC research team: John Purcell, Sue Hutchinson, Bruce Rayton and Konstantinos Georgiades.

Foreword

Once again we have been able to draw on the data generated and reported in the CIPD research report *Understanding the People and Performance Link – Unlocking the black box* to discuss one of the major issues identified by the research. Carried out over a three-year period in eighteen organisations, six of which were in the knowledge-intensive sector, this research offers major insights into the role of people management in bringing about enhanced business performance.

The management of professional knowledge workers and in particular the conversion by organisations of their knowledge and expertise into marketable products and services was one of the key factors underpinning business success in knowledge-intensive situations. This Executive Briefing examines the issue and the people management policies and processes that can assist in the conversion, and enable organisations to deal successfully with some of the critical dilemmas they face in the management of professional knowledge workers.

The people and performance research has resulted in an extraordinarily rich database of attitudinal data, much of which is still to be explored and analysed. This has enabled us to carry out additional analysis in areas of particular interest to increase understanding of the people management–business performance relationship.

As a result, this is the second in a series of Executive Briefings which the CIPD plans to publish exploring in greater depth some of the issues raised by the people and performance work. The first examined the role of the front-line managers, and the third will examine the issue of vision and values, and how these underpin the processes that deliver business performance.

By delving more deeply into the issues that seem to have a major impact on the relationship between people management and business performance, we hope to offer insights to practitioners and enable them to more successfully implement the results of this extensive research programme.

Angela Baron
Adviser, Organisation and Resourcing
Chartered Institute of Personnel and Development

Executive summary

This Briefing explores the ways in which people management policies and processes can contribute to the success of knowledge-intensive organisations that rely heavily on their human capital. In particular, it focuses on the key policies and processes associated with managing the careers of professional knowledge workers who are employed by these organisations.

There is a series of key findings:

◪ Knowledge-intensive organisations and professional knowledge workers have a number of distinct characteristics which make people management issues critical to firm performance.

◪ The success of knowledge-intensive organisations is dependent upon their ability to convert their human capital – the knowledge, skills and experience of their employees – into intellectual capital: the products and services that have value in the marketplace.

◪ The effectiveness of this conversion process depends on the extent to which knowledge-intensive situations and professional knowledge workers are managed successfully.

◪ There are three key knowledge-intensive situations:

– the creation and development of knowledge

– the sharing of knowledge within the organisation

– the sharing of knowledge between organisations.

◪ Professional workers have the following, specific characteristics:

– They need to apply highly structured technical knowledge to ambiguous client demands.

– They work in an autonomous fashion within fluid leadership structures.

– They are normally ambitious and upwardly mobile, and their key focus is the development of their own careers.

◪ The need to pay close attention both to managing knowledge-intensive situations and professional knowledge workers creates three important dilemmas which must be successfully resolved:

- between the retention of knowledge and knowledge workers and the desire of knowledge workers to increase their employability

- between the need to develop organisationally specific knowledge and the wish of knowledge workers to develop transferable knowledge

- between the need for the firm to appropriate the value of that knowledge and the desire by workers to retain their ownership of that knowledge.

◘ Our understanding of these dilemmas is improved by adopting an identity perspective. There are four competing sources of identity for professional knowledge workers:

- professional

- organisational

- team

- client.

◘ Careful attention must be paid to developing people management policies and processes that allow these identities to be managed in ways that are well suited to conditions for the success of these organisations.

◘ This points to the need for mutually reinforcing processes for managing knowledge-intensive situations and professional knowledge workers within these organisations.

1 | Introduction and context

The rise of the knowledge economy has attracted increasing attention to the people management issues associated with managing professional knowledge workers. Many organisations now rely almost exclusively on their human capital – the knowledge and skills of their employees – for gaining a competitive advantage. The key to maintaining the quality of this human capital is the retention and development of employees with scarce and inimitable skills. Managing the careers of professional knowledge workers in such a way that ensures *both* the development *and* the retention of these core skills is therefore fundamental to the success of organisations in the knowledge economy.

This Briefing examines the people management issues associated with the careers of professional knowledge workers. We focus on the key dilemmas that firms experience in this area and illustrate some of the different approaches that are adopted to resolve these tensions. We draw on research conducted for the CIPD that investigated how and why people management policies influence organisational performance. One of the key outcomes of this research was the development of the 'People and Performance' model that highlighted both the key people

management policies and the processes that were critical to their successful implementation.[1]

This wider project studied eighteen organisations in both the private and public sectors, including six organisations in the software industry, together with a number of others that employed substantial numbers of professional employees in fields such as research and development, accounting, consulting and the health service. Our focus here on professional knowledge workers allows us to look inside the generic model we have developed to examine in fine detail the people management policies and processes that are of particular importance for these employees.

> *'... critical to the conversion of human capital into intellectual capital ... are the creation and development of knowledge and the sharing of that knowledge.'*

We set the context for the study by outlining the characteristics of professional knowledge workers and the knowledge-intensive firms that employ them. This is followed, in Chapter 2, by a careful examination of the 'knowledge-intensive situations' critical to the conversion of human capital into intellectual capital which has value in the marketplace. These are the creation and development of knowledge and the sharing of that knowledge within and between organisations.

Building on this, we consider three dilemmas linked to the overarching tension between managing these knowledge-intensive situations and managing the needs of professional employees. These dilemmas have to be managed successfully if the potential of both the knowledge-intensive firm and the professional knowledge workers is to be realised.

In Chapter 4 we consider how these dilemmas can be resolved by using an identity perspective. We examine the different sources of identity for professional knowledge workers, how these interrelate and change over time, and how they affect the careers of employees.

In the final chapter we discuss the people management practices that can be used to manage the various identities successfully and that ultimately enable knowledge-intensive firms to develop and retain their key human capital.

The remainder of this chapter explores the key characteristics of professional knowledge workers and their employing firms. In particular we consider why the management of the careers of professional knowledge workers is so important to the success of the organisations for which they work.

Characteristics of professional knowledge workers

A variety of professional workers can be identified. We are particularly interested in those whom we refer to as professional knowledge workers. These employees are distinguished by the nature of their work, which requires high levels of knowledge input in a non-routinised manner where the subsequent output results in a product or service within which their knowledge is embedded (Alvesson, 2001; page 1103)

Professional knowledge workers can be contrasted with traditional, highly regulated and highly routinised professions such as accounting. These professions are governed by a code of ethics and have restricted access and constraints placed on them by a professional community.

The kind of employees we are particularly interested in – software workers, research and development employees, and more creative employees – are not governed by these kinds of institutions and principles. These professionals have to create new knowledge through the application of highly developed theoretical frameworks to unknown practical problems. Such employees have been regarded as 'aspirant professionals' (Von Glinow, 1988) and they have a number of characteristics that are central to our discussion.

- First, it is not just the presence of human capital in an organisation that is important so much as the ability to convert this into intellectual capital which has value in the marketplace. There is often heavy reliance on tacit knowledge rather than formal procedures. Much of the work these employees are engaged in is highly ambiguous. Questions are posed, frequently by clients, that are not only often poorly defined but also have ambiguous outcomes, in the sense that whether these are good or bad answers often depends on what the client thinks.

◘ Second, these problems are essentially non-repetitive and usually require novel and bespoke answers. Although there may be precedents which can be found, each problem tends to involve a unique combination of events placing a premium on initiative and innovation. Many of these employees work exceptionally long hours, where commitment is related more to the nature of the work (for example, designing an exceptional system) than to the organisation. They have a strong sense of intrinsic motivation and are mostly interested in challenging work (Swart, Kinnie and Purcell, 2003).

◘ Third, professional knowledge workers also tend to identify with other professionals rather than with the organisation for which they work (Von Glinow, 1988) and therefore develop strong interpersonal networks that span organisational boundaries. They are also often young and upwardly mobile and tend to move frequently between various career opportunities. They often share a sense of professionalism without formally being governed by a professional body.

◘ It is these employees who have been recognised as enjoying a 'boundary-less career' with high levels of career mobility compared, for example, with other professionals (Arthur and Rousseau, 1996). Lawyers and accountants have been portrayed as much more immobile, spending perhaps the whole of their working lives in the single firm in which they did their training, with the aim of making it to partner one day. There are, however, some signs that this may be changing, perhaps because the promise of partnership is not as realistic as it once was.

◘ These employees have scarce skills that are generic and therefore easily transferable between organisations. Indeed, as we shall see, the very nature of their cross-boundary work actually encourages this movement. The ability of these employees to move frequently is, of course, market-dependent, and recent changes – for example, in the software industry – have led to a slowing down in this mobility.

> '... *professional knowledge workers ... tend to identify with other professionals rather than with the organisation for which they work.*'

◘ Finally, 'career-hopping' is often facilitated and stimulated by the membership of external professional networks made up of like-minded people. These may be based on the networks to which their employing organisation belongs, where employees come into contact with suppliers and clients; at other times they may be completely independent of the employer. These may draw on semi-formal networks such as groupings of university alumni or professional associations, or perhaps be based on conferences and interactive websites.

◘ Professional employees belong to these networks for a variety of purposes. They may be for professional development as a way of keeping up to date in the field, as a source of business for their employer (suppliers may become clients and vice versa), or as a way of finding employment opportunities or new potential employees. In some organisations, as we shall see, professional knowledge workers are also members of internal networks made up of loosely structured, fluid project teams.

The key points for our discussion are that professional knowledge workers are often engaged in non-repetitive bespoke work using skills and knowledge which are scarce but vital to the success of their firms, and they have access to multiple career paths because of the nature of their work. We will consider the implications of this in more detail in the next chapter, once we have considered the characteristics of their employing organisations.

Characteristics of the employing organisation

There are a variety of settings in which professional knowledge workers are employed: in departments of large companies, in knowledge-intensive firms that supply larger organisations, or on a self-employed, contract basis. We are particularly interested in the second of these, the knowledge-intensive firms (KIFs), where the majority of employees are professional knowledge workers, as opposed to other, larger organisations where these workers may make up only a small proportion of the overall workforce.

We are especially interested in these because we feel they bring into focus many of the problems and issues that are at the heart of people management in this area. However, many of the problems and issues we discuss apply equally to those employed in departments of larger organisations. Indeed, we might argue that many of the changes taking place in larger organisations – such as the total quality movement, in which internal customers are identified and which involves the close integration of supply chains with the customer and client – have led to large firms and their supplier companies becoming more similar.

These KIFs tend to be small to medium-sized and include software houses, research and development firms, consultants, and creative organisations such as those in advertising and the media. Their characteristic work processes, work organisation and external relations hold particular implications for the management of professionals (See Appendix for further details).

Work processes

Knowledge has particular importance for these firms, compared with physical and financial capital. At the heart of the business model of the KIFs is the conversion of the knowledge, skills and experience of their people into intellectual capital in the form of products and services that are tangible and have value in the marketplace. Ideally, they wish to embed knowledge and skills to create distinctive products and services, and therefore maximise their knowledge development investment.

Work organisation

These firms organise their work around project teams that centre on either a particular client or a specific process. Teams may work together for different periods: some are established for a few days, whereas others last up to a few months or perhaps longer. The teams are often multi-disciplinary, with a changing membership composition based on the needs of the project. The multi-disciplinary nature of the members often presents knowledge-sharing challenges in itself because the members 'speak different languages'. Such teams tend to be assigned to a particular client and may meet physically or be virtual teams. As we discuss in the next chapter, this form of work organisation can have a negative impact on the development of new skills, yet it is the key method used to meet client deadlines. Employees are often required to work very long hours using their expert skills in order to see a project through to completion.

External relations

Many of these firms – especially the very small KIFs – are dependent upon only a small number of clients in the larger network with whom they are engaged in business-to-business relationships. The relationships with these clients are nurtured over time and are often very strong and central to the firm's success. Such close relationships mean that professional employees work on the client site perhaps for extended periods of time.

> '*Ideally, [KIFs] wish to embed knowledge and skills to ... maximise their knowledge development investment.*'

These firms also work in close partnership with other organisations as part of a network of links that includes clients, suppliers, short-term collaborators, and longer-term partners and alliances. Such networks are critical to the success of the organisation, and the performance of any one firm in the network can be understood only in the context of the network as a whole. Prominent in the network configuration of the KIF is its knowledge networks: knowledge and skills are often exchanged across traditional organisational boundaries, or new cross-boundary teams are established to work on particular projects.

Figures 1 and 2 (overleaf) illustrate the kinds of network we are discussing.

Figure 1 | Bespoke Ware network

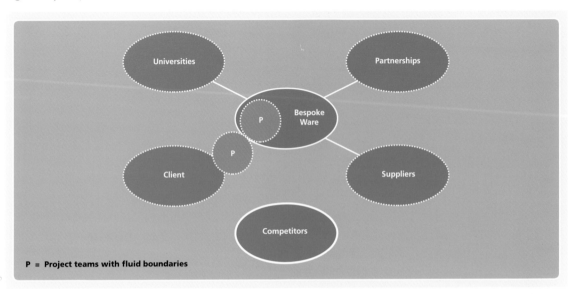

Figure 2 | FinSoft network

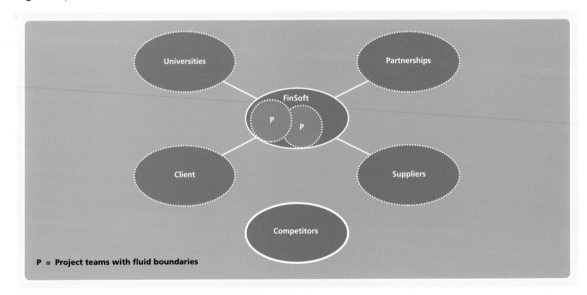

To sum up, although professional knowledge workers are widely employed, we are particularly interested in those whose work is non-repetitive, requiring a high level of skill application to bespoke services and products. Furthermore, these professional knowledge workers are employed by firms who are internally organised into project teams and have permeable organisational boundaries. This allows knowledge to flow throughout the networks of firms to which they belong.

The combination of this particular type of professional knowledge worker and the characteristics of the firms that employ them creates sets of tensions between managing knowledge and managing knowledge workers. What the firm may need and want does not always align with the knowledge needs of its employees.

We consider the specific knowledge needs of the firm in Chapter 2, where we examine the specific knowledge-intensive situations that are vital to the development of intellectual capital. Thereafter we juxtapose the knowledge needs of the firms and the employee, and illustrate that the opposing needs present specific dilemmas that have to be resolved if the firm is to retain and develop its human capital.

Endnote

1   The other members of the research team were John Purcell, Sue Hutchinson and Bruce Rayton. For further information on these projects see Purcell *et al* (2003) and Swart *et al* (2003).

2 | Converting human capital into intellectual capital: knowledge-intensive situations

In the previous chapter we described the context for our study in terms of the characteristics of professional knowledge workers and the firms that employ them. Here we present the specific knowledge needs of the firm and develop an understanding of the ways in which knowledge creates a competitive advantage for these firms. In short, what are the processes critical to the conversion of human capital into intellectual capital that can create a competitive advantage?

We identify three knowledge-intensive situations in which the processes vital to the conversion of human capital are most important:

◻ the enhancement of knowledge creation and knowledge flow through learning-by-doing – the focal point is the *knowledge worker and the project* or knowledge-intensive work itself

◻ knowledge-sharing within the organisation where the quality of boundaries influences the knowledge-sharing process – this focuses on knowledge flow through practice and *conversations between the knowledge worker and the team and between teams*

◻ knowledge-sharing between the organisation, its partners (if they exist) and the client, where again the quality of boundaries influences the knowledge-sharing process – this focuses on knowledge flow through practice and *conversations between the organisation and its clients and any network members*.

Knowledge creation through learning-by-doing

Most knowledge workers agree that knowledge-intensive work starts by 'figuring things out by yourself', 'trying different paths to a solution' and 'learning from your own mistakes'. A great deal of knowledge creation takes place on the individual level, where each knowledge worker engages with and in knowledge work before knowledge-sharing is possible.

Nonaka and Takeuchi (1995) argue that knowledge creation starts with the investment in tacit knowledge where learning takes place through doing, active engagement/practice and reflection, and asking questions about practice. It is through tacit skill accumulation that the human capital is strengthened within the organisation. Thus the first step in the knowledge-creating spiral is where tacit skill is shared through practice and then formalised through organisational routines that serve as a context within which new employees acquire these organisation-specific tacit skills (see Figure 3).

Collective knowledge-sharing originates at the individual level, within the act of problem-solution and learning. Although many organisations do this, our KIFs actively invested time in these knowledge processes. Continuous learning was driven by the organisational culture and actively enacted by professional knowledge workers every day: it was part of the 'way of thinking' in the successful KIFs. Employees were given redundant time[1] to develop new software development skills by 'messing about on the Internet' or 'trying new things to see how they worked', or to 'try different solutions to current client work' in order to develop individual tacit skills. As one of our respondents said:

We learn mainly on the job, but we have to support each other and learn from each other as well.

Individual tacit skill accumulation was also supported by formalised mentoring and

Figure 3 | The knowledge-creating spiral with tacit skill accumulation as its focus

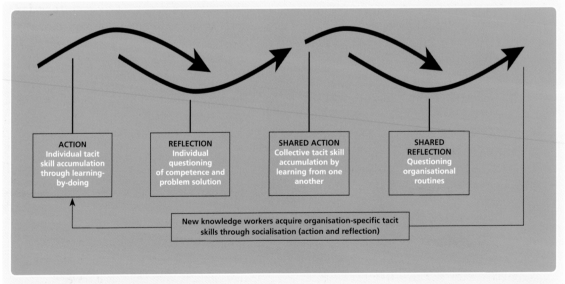

Source: adapted from Nonaka and Takeuchi, 1995

performance management systems which were used to encourage learning and enforce the behavioural norms. This is where the collective tacit skill accumulation cuts across the individual level of learning. It is important to learn new software codes/methods of synthesis, but it will only be valuable to the organisation if the new skills are applied to projects in the organisation and become specific to the organisation, thereby creating a competitive advantage.

A knowledge worker who uses redundant time to acquire valuable skills needs to apply them to writing software which then translates into chargeable action. These skills must be shared with other software engineers to give the organisation as a whole an advantage over its competitors. Likewise, a student engineer who has cutting-edge technical knowledge must learn organisation-specific ways of skill application before the knowledge can be translated into intellectual capital in knowledge-intensive processes.

The key point about learning individually through reflection on the project or acquiring organisation-specific skills through observing others is that the behavioural dimensions of the skills cannot be verbalised. Our respondents emphasised that only experience can serve as a foundation for competence – it was through the *application* of technical knowledge that you and other knowledge workers around you would learn.

Taught training courses were therefore of little value, and it was only the sharing of experience in different communities within the organisation and with the client that laid a solid foundation for knowledge creation. Participants commented that you could not tell someone how to do something: it was through doing things together that you could learn more.

Knowledge-sharing within organisations

Knowledge creation depends partly on the effectiveness of knowledge-sharing processes within the organisation. Knowledge-sharing was most likely to be effective when it had the following characteristics:

◘ It was a continuous process and not just one-off question-answering.

◘ The sharing of information was combined with practice – showing fellow knowledge workers how to practise a skill – or intermittent advice given during the application of a skill.

◘ It was grounded upon a shared understanding of the skill developed by working together closely over an extended period of time.

> *'... only experience can serve as a foundation for competence ...'*

Knowledge-sharing could take place in different parts of the firm. Firstly, most organisations developed skills and shared problem solutions within a *project team* because this was often the most important day-to-day work situation for many employees. The importance of these was demonstrated through the physical layout (members of the project team would be seated in close proximity or at one laboratory bay) and the frequency of interaction. Knowledge workers in one project team often engaged in conversation about a particular problem, stood huddled over a single computer screen giving opinions about a possible solution, or emailed one another asking questions relating to difficulties with the project. Project teams often set the social as well as professional boundaries as team members engaged in work conversations after hours.

Secondly, there are opportunities for knowledge-sharing *between project teams*. In a few of our cases the project team boundaries appeared to be very solid: there was little interaction with other teams and employees felt isolated and frustrated because they were not learning new skills. Having weak relationships between project teams was a barrier to success in knowledge-intensive processes. In the words of two of our respondents:

There are people to ask, but you need to let people know who to ask.

I don't know what goes on in other project teams.

> **'Where [boundaries] were permeable, knowledge flowed freely and technical development time was reduced significantly.'**

Strong links between various employees in an internal knowledge network serves as a map/guidebook for 'knowing who to ask' when skills development is needed. Most of our participants believed that the heart of internal knowledge-sharing processes was the ability to identify experts in an organisation who can then be approached with technical questions. This process can also be referred to as the building of social capital, where relationships are developed between employees and where these relationships serve a developmental function in the organisation, thereby linking social capital to organisational competence. Various barriers – such as the time needed to identify experts, the size of the organisation and an internal focus within a project team – made it difficult to build the necessary social capital. As one respondent said:

What is important is knowing where the expertise lies.

Boundaries between teams influenced knowledge-sharing. Where they were permeable, knowledge flowed freely and technical development time was reduced significantly. Impermeable boundaries, however, led to the hoarding of knowledge within a project team and a reinvention of the wheel each time the organisation received similar project work.

The team boundaries were more permeable when there was a commitment to employee development and participation in decision-making. These values were represented by having structures in place that overlapped with the project team structure – for example, the establishment of a working group responsible for strategic decisions that includes members from several project teams, or a mentoring system by which a mentor is involved in the development of employees from other project teams. Multi-boundary and multi-project team structures made team boundaries more permeable and encouraged knowledge flow throughout the organisation.

FinSoft recognised the importance of this and established a multiple team structure in which employees typically belonged to four types of team simultaneously:

- their project team, which was based around a client or product
- their vocational team, in which employees such as testers would get together to discuss issues of common concern
- their communications team, which was responsible for sharing information upward and downward in the organisation
- their various social and sporting teams.

This multiple team structure was effective in weakening the project team boundaries and encouraging knowledge-sharing between teams.

Technological and interpersonal networks often supported these knowledge-sharing processes. Some organisations had an intranet on which employees recorded their latest technical interest, new skills they had developed, and details of projects in progress and workload. These software tools were successful in facilitating knowledge-sharing only if interpersonal knowledge networks were already in place and used frequently. Where only technology was used to manage knowledge flow, the intranet was simply not understood, accepted or used, causing greater cynicism on the part of knowledge workers towards management-initiated knowledge-sharing projects. Formal mechanisms for knowledge-sharing thus reflected rather than overcame these internal boundaries.

Knowledge-sharing between project teams can therefore only be successful if it is a natural way of working or is embedded in the organisational routines. It needs to be a practice accepted and developed by knowledge workers, rather than a policy imposed from above by a management team. Our participants believed that knowledge work could not be conducted in any other way – sharing what you know and asking others is implicit in knowledge-intensive work. This points to the need to question barriers in organisations where knowledge flow is hindered, and it highlights the deep-rooted nature of these barriers.

Knowledge-sharing between organisations

KIFs often work for a relatively small number of clients, and sometimes alongside other suppliers. They ideally seek stable, long-term, high-value-added contracts which take full advantage of their intellectual capital. The quality of their knowledge of the industry and potential clients and the relevant knowledge-sharing processes are vital to their success.

> *'... where the boundaries ... are impermeable, ... employees are left investing longer periods of time ... sometimes without a successful outcome.'*

KIFs typically gain contracts by being invited to tender for business or to prepare a proposal for a project. Before this, however, they have to establish a reputation in the industry for their type of work. This might be by making formal presentations, publishing research reports or gaining publicity through successful reference sites. More simply, they become known in the industry through informal knowledge-sharing channels for having expertise in a certain field and attract business because of this – for example, for the ability to tackle certain types of problem and develop solutions. Once their reputation is established, they are in a good position to develop a trusting relationship with their clients.

When an invitation to bid has been received, the problem must be diagnosed and a proposal prepared. However, the problem itself may be ambiguous. As one of our software engineers put it:

Sometimes you will get a call from a client who has a very vague idea of what they want. They don't know what to expect from you, and you are not clear about how your skills can be used to solve their problem.

Knowledge-sharing in this context involves negotiation with the potential client to reduce the ambiguity and construct a project specification. In the absence of this negotiation process, where the boundaries between the KIF and the client are impermeable, ambiguity remains high and the employees are left investing longer periods of time on a project, producing several versions of a solution, sometimes without a successful outcome.

This emphasises the importance of client involvement in knowledge-sharing, which helps to build the trust between the KIF and its client that is essential for recognising competence and developing professional respect (Baumard, 1999; Bontis, 1998; Leonard-Barton, 1995; Nonaka, 1994). Even if the problem is clear-cut, the preparation of a proposal will severely test the internal knowledge-sharing processes as well as the skills and knowledge of individual employees, especially where time is short. There is a need to draw together expertise from previous projects and other sources of market research and intelligence.

If the contract is awarded, a project team will be assembled to work either full-time dedicated to that client or part-time alongside work for other clients. The critical issues at this point are managing relations between the client, the project team and the wider KIF organisation. Relations with clients have to be managed, including understanding and responding to their needs and keeping them up to date with progress. Contact may be with one or multiple parts of the client, depending on the size of the project. Indeed, in large, complex projects the supplying KIF may effectively be providing a means of internal knowledge-sharing for the client as it pieces together the disparate parts of their internal organisation.

Client relationships may be managed through a single, senior contact such as a project manager or director, or through a variety of senior and junior staff. These client relationship roles require the ability to be both client-facing and project-team-facing, to be able to translate and reconcile the requests of the client and the wishes of the members of the project team. Client requests, or demands, may place enormous strain on project teams, especially if they change at short notice.

These relations may be managed jointly by a hybrid team made up of employees from the client and the supplying KIF. Sometimes these hybrid teams form a strong identity such that the boundaries between the different organisations virtually, but not completely, disappear. Indeed, one danger here is that members of this hybrid team will form such a close-knit group that they become isolated from their employing organisations. This creates barriers to sharing knowledge within the KIF.

KIFs also collaborate informally or formally with various other partners. For example, informal collaboration might be through networks of contacts linked to higher education or professional associations. These informal, external knowledge networks provide the opportunity for updating industry knowledge vital to gaining new business.

Sharing knowledge through friends and colleagues who happen to be working for other firms seems quite natural, especially where there is a shared disciplinary background, such as chemistry, or a common software language. A 'collegial' atmosphere develops, often supported by various social links, which easily permeates organisational boundaries. These informal networks are also supplemented by market research and other secondary data-gathering activities from written and electronic sources.

More formal collaboration between suppliers is sometimes requested by some clients. Indeed, KIFs may be required to work together to produce a seamless product or service for the client. This kind of co-operation does not always come easily between organisations that are effectively competitors. However, the demands of the client require the partners to co-operate so that they break down the organisational boundaries that are barriers to knowledge-sharing. Concerns over intellectual property rights and commercial confidentiality provide further obstacles to the knowledge-sharing required. This necessitates a high degree of trust between the partners, which usually takes a long time to develop.

> *'... informal external knowledge networks provide the opportunity for updating industry knowledge vital to gaining new business.'*

In summary, we have identified three knowledge-intensive situations that are critical to the process of converting the human capital of a firm, held by its employees, into intellectual capital that creates a competitive advantage. We consider the management of these knowledge creation and sharing situations to be a core competence and central to the performance of the organisation. However, the management of these knowledge-intensive situations is not the only concern of KIFs. Parallel to developing their knowledge management core competence they must consider the aims of the creators and sharers of this knowledge: their professional knowledge workers.

We now turn our attention to the tensions that exist between managing knowledge-intensive situations and managing professional knowledge workers.

Endnote

1 'Redundant time' was time that was set aside for self-managed skill development accounted for under chargeable hours but not billed to a particular client.

3 | Managing knowledge and managing professional knowledge workers

The creation of intellectual capital depends not only on the competent management of the firm's knowledge but also on the effective management of professional knowledge workers' careers. The firm has to create and enable knowledge-sharing while retaining key individuals whose knowledge has value in a competitive market. There are times, however, when the interests of the knowledge worker and those of the firm can pull in different directions. The tension between addressing the needs of individual professional knowledge workers and the need to manage knowledge within the firm is examined in detail in this chapter.

This tension was neatly summed up by the human capital director in one of our case studies, who said:

My real challenge is to retain and develop my people.

Keeping and developing professional knowledge workers would allow the intellectual capital essential to the firm's success to be maximised. Solving the retention-development tension would avoid a problem common to many organisations

– that they risk losing employees before they have had a chance to capture the value from their development. Most organisations seek to maximise their investment in the development of human capital by erecting mobility barriers to prevent the loss of key staff (Seely Brown, 2002).

We identify three particular dilemmas that emerge from the overarching tension between the need to manage knowledge and also to manage knowledge workers, as shown in Figure 4 (overleaf).

The first of the dilemmas contrasts the desire of some professionals to move between employers with the need of the organisation to retain its talent. The second concerns how the organisation and the individual view their development needs: whereas the organisation needs to create and embed unique skills in order to compete effectively, the professional may prefer to focus on developing transferable skills and knowledge. The final dilemma centres on the appropriation of knowledge: both the firm and the professional may feel a high sense of ownership over knowledge inputs and outputs alike. This may lead to excessive demands made on the professional to 'give up' his or her 'right' to own the knowledge outputs.

The retention–employability dilemma

The ability to create knowledge and apply it to client solutions sits at the heart of a successful KIF. This is, however, not the only dimension of competence that has to be developed in order to compete. It is critical that the knowledge which the firm develops is retained within the organisation both collectively and individually.

Collective retention can be achieved by embedding knowledge into the daily routines (Nelson and Winter, 1987), which resembles firm-level know-how or organisation-specific knowledge. For instance, DataWare had a specific process for dealing with client demands that was developed over time and eventually provided the firm with the ability to compete against larger firms. Collective knowledge retention is dependent upon the processes used historically as well as the introduction of new processes through individual employees within the firm. The balance between preservation and renewal (March, 1991) enables

Figure 4 | Managing knowledge and professional knowledge workers: key dilemmas

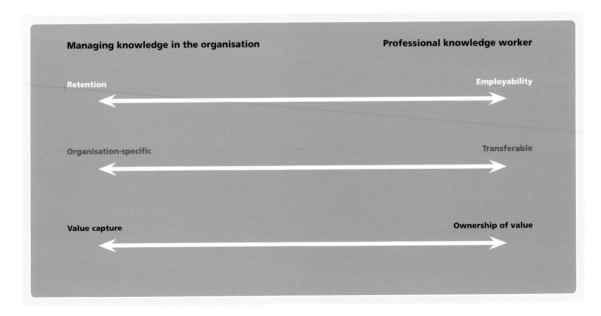

the firm to turn human capital into intellectual capital in the current timeframe, and it also prepares the firm to compete in the future.

It is important to explore the processes that sit behind the preservation–renewal dimension of the firm in order to understand what makes a firm successful. A closer look at the integration of preservation and renewal highlights the specific links between the individual and collective levels of knowledge. The individual professional knowledge worker often brings about pockets of renewal in the firm, whereas the preservation of these changes mainly takes place at the collective level as it becomes embedded in the firm. For this reason, it is important not only that the firm provides its employees with challenging opportunities of knowledge creation but that the individuals are retained within the firm in order to bring about the renewal of firm-level processes.

Retention of knowledge can also be exclusively at the level of the individual employee. In other words, not all individual know-how can be absorbed and embedded within the firm, and there will always be pockets of knowledge that remain with a particular professional knowledge worker (see box on p.23). Previous research indicates that it is not possible to share all forms of individual knowledge (Baumard, 1999; Nonaka and Takeuchi, 1995; Polanyi, 1966; Swart *et al*, 2003), and that within specific power relations in a firm a professional knowledge worker may choose not to share individual knowledge. A considerable proportion of knowledge therefore

remains within the control and ownership of the individual. Within a knowledge economy where competitive advantage is knowledge-based, the individual's knowledge is often particularly valuable to a firm and constitutes the key advantage over their competitors.

As an employee in Chemlab said:

Nothing can beat experience – for example, picking up throw-away lines in journals, seeing products you can do something about, understanding the drug company attitudes, and knowing how to negotiate.

> '**it is important ... that [knowledge workers] are retained within the firm in order to bring about the renewal of firm-level processes.**'

The retention of these employees is therefore critically important, and tends to be demonstrated most clearly when things go wrong and key staff leave.[1] This can have serious direct financial implications associated with the lost investment in training and development and the replacement costs. Losing key staff may also impair the firm's ability to deliver the services promised to a client or the product developments needed to compete in the marketplace.

The ability to retain both collective and individual knowledge can therefore be regarded as a core competence of a KIF. The investment in knowledge creation must generate the return of applying knowledge to client problems and retaining the knowledge within the boundaries of the firm for future value appropriation. This may of course stand in direct contrast to the needs of the individual knowledge worker.

The key interest of the individual knowledge worker is employability (Cappelli, 1999; Valcour and Snell, 2002). In the software industry in particular it is common practice to move between employers every 18 to 36 months (Labour Force Survey, 2000). The *raison d'être* of the employee is to build a curriculum vitae that illustrates his or her ability to master cutting-edge skills and shows that he or she can apply them in a variety of settings. Knowledge workers are looking to develop their careers in novel and interesting ways, and in some industries it is known that this goal cannot be achieved by remaining with one employer for an extended period of time. Furthermore, the ability to move between employers is an accepted standard that is often taken as an indication of exceptional ability on the part of the employee. In the interests of career development the professional knowledge worker will seek to push against the retention need of the KIF and build a career that maximises his or her employability.

We label this challenge the 'retention-employability dilemma'. If an organisation fails to address and manage this dilemma, it will lose its valuable staff and its ability to compete effectively. The second dilemma follows on from the knowledge-creation aspect of the retention–employability question and asks whether employees and employers have similar *skill development* needs.

The development focus dilemma

Organisations seek to differentiate themselves by offering unique services or products for which they can charge premium prices. In order to do this they need their employees to develop organisation-specific skills (Swart, Kinnie and Purcell, 2003). One way this can be done is to form close working relationships with their clients and expose their employees to problem-solution processes that are unique to the organisation. They also develop their own unique products and services and organisational routines which employees must follow. Thus the specific client relationships and the content of the knowledge-intensive service or product determines how the organisation-specific skills are configured.

In essence, the knowledge-based competition is built upon a slow transfer of skills between competitors. As with knowledge retention, this has both an individual and collective knowledge dimension: firms compete for unique individual skills, a scarce resource known as expert knowledge, and firm processes must be inimitable in order to provide a sustainable competitive advantage.

Professional knowledge workers, on the other hand, aim to develop transferable skills that will make them attractive to prospective employers. They may seek to achieve this in a variety of ways. They may prefer to work with client problems that will develop transferable skills and in turn meet their employability needs. This might include

Chemlab competes for human capital (skills and knowledge) in life sciences, and in particular, neurochemistry. The firm therefore has a high level of unique, individual skills that can be applied only within this particular firm. Furthermore, it has developed a specific way in which it builds client relationships and combines various areas of chemistry, which relates to the organisational level of inimitable processes. It is important to know that the individual chemists who carry out these processes would probably not be able to use their skills within another competing firm.

working with the latest technology or being required to solve particularly complex problems. Alternatively, they may simply want access to the latest training courses in order to maintain their accreditation, which in turn increases their attractiveness to other employers or enhances their ability to work on a self-employed basis. If a firm mainly develops organisation-specific skills, the employee may sacrifice his or her employability need. Firms therefore need to strike a balance within their skill development agenda between organisation-specific and transferable skills, which in turn has an impact on their approach to the management of the careers of professional knowledge workers.

This dilemma is especially evident when professional knowledge workers are asked to take on line or general management responsibilities. Indeed, in some organisations the only way to gain promotion over a certain level is to become a team leader or manager. Typically, this will entail responsibility for managing staff, including recruitment and performance appraisal. In this way the firm is looking to develop the employee in non-technical ways to benefit the organisation specifically.

Some employees have little interest in this kind of activity – indeed, they may resent it and see such people management activities as unnecessary obstacles to doing 'real' work which uses the skills developed through their training and experience. Consequently, they will carry out their tasks, if at all, in an uncommitted and amateurish way, presenting severe problems for all involved.

The value appropriation dilemma

KIFs rely on the knowledge and skills of their employees – but they have to create the ideal situations for this knowledge to be developed and shared. The simultaneous developing and sharing of knowledge present a management challenge in itself because professional workers are often keen to hold on to their knowledge in order to secure their next career opportunity, be that within or outside the organisation. Furthermore, the employers need to retain the valuable knowledge that has been developed in order to create further value from their investment.

'Firms ... need to strike a balance within their skill development agenda between organisation-specific and transferable skills ...'

This represents a *value appropriation dilemma*. In short, the firm needs to appropriate value or high rents (Blyer and Coff, 2003) from the knowledge developed. The process of value capture is, however, not as clearly defined in knowledge-based firms as in traditional firms because the capital which generates rents – ie human capital – does not have clear ownership boundaries. Both the professional worker and the firm may feel that they have a right to capture value from the knowledge outputs. The professional knowledge worker will take pride in his or her acquisition and application of knowledge. Such workers are likely to have studied over a long period, perhaps at their own expense and in their own time, and will feel that they own this knowledge. At the same time, this knowledge is at the core of the business model which involves turning human capital into intellectual capital delivering products and services that clients want. Nonetheless, the professional may lay claim to the knowledge outputs, claiming that the firm could not have generated the products or services without him or her.

If the firm is to appropriate value from its employees, the issue is not just of retention, as discussed earlier, but retaining the right kinds of employee and keeping them interested and motivated. Knowledge work involves a high degree of discretionary activity, and employees must be motivated to perform consistently to their highest standards. The main way of doing that, of course, is to provide them with interesting work, which is itself dependent upon being able to obtain interesting work from clients in the first place.

Human capital, within these firms, therefore falls within a continuum along which both the firm and the individual has a sense of ownership and right to appropriate value or rents. Once again, the interests of the individual and the firm could pull in opposite directions, and employees may react to this tension by negotiating with the organisation to make it attractive for them to retain their knowledge within the boundaries of the firm. For example, a software engineer may demand higher wages because it is difficult to replace him or her. The firm must therefore minimise the risk of excessive appropriation by the professional workers themselves. It must guard against excessive pay demands or the leaking of knowledge (in terms both of innovation and of clients) when the employees leave the firm by erecting resource mobility barriers (Mueller, 1996).

Yet throughout this process it is important for firms to satisfy the career needs of their employees by encouraging them to remain with the organisation, thereby reducing the career mobility across organisational boundaries. When an organisation is solely reliant upon its human capital, the risk associated with frequent career moves between organisations is far greater, because the inability to manage the leaking of knowledge across boundaries can adversely affect the firm.

The development and negotiation of mobility barriers is often made more difficult because of the relatively permeable boundaries between the firm and its external network ties (Swart and Kinnie, 2003). The KIF has frequent interaction between clients, partners, educators and suppliers at many levels in the organisation, and knowledge tends to flow relatively freely across these boundaries. Professional workers are therefore exposed to various employment practices through their client and professional networks and are very well aware of the demands they could make of their employers. Furthermore, knowledge will flow freely across the network boundaries through the process of delivering a knowledge-intensive output or service. By nature, this complicates the value appropriation process further and presents the employer with additional challenges in respect of knowledge and employee retention.

The career management perspective

The three dilemmas described here represent different aspects of the tension between managing knowledge and managing knowledge workers. The firm needs to create, develop and embed knowledge and, by implication, manage its knowledge assets while simultaneously providing opportunities for cutting-edge skill development. Within the development focus dilemma, knowledge worker expectations must be met through the growth of transferable skills while at the same time enhancing firm-specific knowledge and embedding this within its knowledge processes. Finally, the firm needs to capture value

from the knowledge development in which it invests, but also needs to provide the means for knowledge workers to perceive that they have a good degree of ownership over their knowledge.

In essence, knowledge management in this context is the very process that enables the conversion from human to intellectual capital. The ability to manage the tension between the firm's own knowledge requirements (knowledge creation, transfer and capture) and the needs of knowledge workers (employability and cutting-edge skill development) is at the heart of this conversion process. Such tension can be resolved by adopting a *career management perspective* which requires a clear understanding of the forces that affect on the professional's career objectives.

The firm has to meet the career objectives of the professional worker and to use this knowledge to compete effectively. That is, the firm must develop and retain knowledge by directing careers in a way that enables both the creation of knowledge and cutting-edge skills and their maximisation through the capture of intellectual capital. This calls for an awareness of the people management practices that will enable professionals to invest in their career in the firm while allowing the firm to capture value from the knowledge generated by its employees.

> *'The firm needs to create, develop and embed knowledge … while simultaneously providing opportunities for cutting-edge skill development.'*

In summary, this chapter set out to explore the various dilemmas that present themselves when seeking to manage both knowledge and professional knowledge workers. These arise when a firm seeks to manage both its own knowledge needs and those of its employees. Such dilemmas include:

◻ the retention–employability dilemma, where the organisation endeavours to retain its key human capital, and this same group of people seeks to build their experience and make themselves more employable by moving frequently between employers

◻ the development focus dilemma, where the organisation endeavours to develop skills that cannot be easily transferred beyond the boundaries of the organisation, whereas the employees aim to develop transferable skills which make them attractive to other organisations

◻ the value appropriation dilemma, where both the organisation and the professional knowledge workers seek to capture value from and have ownership over the knowledge products and processes that are generated.

In the following chapter we use the concept of *identity* to help us understand how these dilemmas or tensions can be managed. We are specifically interested in how competing identities can be managed by the firm.

Endnote

1   There are, of course, some situations where a certain level of labour turnover might be regarded as necessary to infuse the organisations with new ideas.

4 | Managing the careers of professional knowledge workers: an identity perspective

The effective management of the careers of professional workers can enable a firm to resolve the tension between developing the knowledge of its employees and retaining its key sources of human capital. Our successful firms were able to obtain high levels of career satisfaction and low levels of labour turnover while investing in the needs of professional workers' career development.

In this chapter we use the concept of *identity* to help us understand the influences on the careers of professional knowledge workers. We highlight four sources of identity for these workers that pull in different directions. If these are not managed carefully, the cost can be high – the professional worker might leave to invest the knowledge developed by the firm with a competitor. We use our cases to illustrate how our firms go about establishing and managing these identities in their efforts to resolve the development–retention dilemma.

Much of the recent interest in the concept of identity has focused on organisational identity, especially the attempts to shape the extent to which employees identify with their employing organisation (Alvesson, 2001; Alvesson and Willmott, 2002; Brown and Starkey, 2000; Hatch and Schultz, 2002; Scott and Lane, 2000). We believe that in professional firms the concept of identity stretches beyond that of organisational identity to include professional, team and client identity.

Types and sources of identity for professional knowledge workers

An employee's need for identification becomes all the more important when neither the organisational hierarchy nor the technology prescribes behaviour in detail (Alvesson, 2000). The work of some professionals – software professionals in particular – is often unstructured, highly tailored to client demands and evolutionary in nature (Morris, 2000; Swart *et al*, 2003). The development of an identity or, indeed, multiple identities is highly significant for professionals, and we argue that a strongly developed identity, or a sense of belonging and loyalty, can influence the subsequent career choices of the individual.

The identity of professionals is developed through interaction with various sources of identity (Ashforth and Mael, 1989; Brown and Starkey, 2000). These professionals are exposed to several competing groups (Brown, 1969) with whom they can identify:

The individual's social identity may be derived not only from the organisation, but also from his or her work group, department, union, lunch group, age cohort, fast-track group, and so on.
Ashforth and Mael, 1989

We believe that four different sources of identity can be recognised from professional knowledge workers, as shown in Figure 5.

◘ *Professional identity* is derived from a variety of sources: employees' initial training, their membership of specialist bodies, attendance at conferences and membership of formal or informal networks. As we outlined in Chapter 1, these range from the formal professional institutions with recognised rules for membership and conduct to much looser arrangements, perhaps based simply on virtual networks reliant on common interests. This will take the form of employees' desire to improve their own knowledge and skills and their ability to improve their career prospects. In our research we have based our assessment of professional identity on the extent to which employees find their job challenging and

Figure 5 | Multiple sources of identity

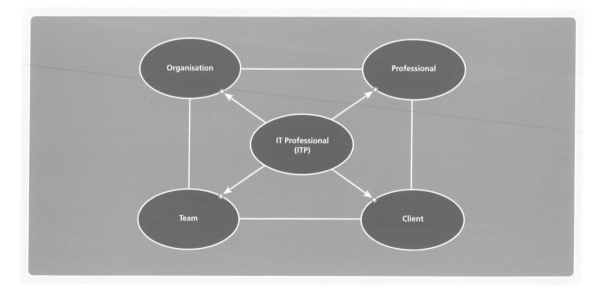

whether they feel the firm makes their work as interesting and varied as possible.

◘ *Organisational identity* is concerned with the loyalty and commitment which the employees display towards the organisation. This may take a variety of forms, including knowledge of and agreement on the goals and culture of the organisation. Evidence of strong organisational identity is to be seen in a willingness to engage in discretionary activity to serve the needs of the firm, such as working considerable overtime without being paid for it. In addition, employees are willing to participate in activities that are not directly related to their own job or careers. Our measures of organisational identity are based on the degree of loyalty to the organisation, the sense of pride and the extent to which the values of the organisation are shared. These scales were combined into a joint measure: 'organisational commitment'.[1]

◘ *Team identity* develops because employees spend much of their working time in their project teams. Indeed, in some instances the team is the principal means by which they experience the organisation: they will have frequent contact with their team leader and other team members but much less involvement with other members of the organisation. Employees will come to know one another well often on a professional and personal level, especially if they are working in a team for several months or even years.

In some instances they will be working away from the organisation's site, increasing their feelings of a shared experience. Team identity is measured through the sense of teamworking, and supporting qualitative data on the strength or sense of teamworking. These data are often referred to as a sense of belonging, helping one another when deadlines are tough, and identifying with one another in a social sense as well.

> '*Our measures of organisational identity are based on the degree of loyalty to the organisation, the sense of pride, and the extent to which the values ... are shared.*'

◘ *Client identity* develops because much of the employee's working time is spent on services for a specific client, either internal or external to an organisation. The employees often have to develop a very close knowledge of the client and its products, procedures and processes. Over this time they may begin to internalise many of the values and ways of working of the client. In common language they can 'go native' and identify strongly with the needs of the client – often because they are under operational day-to-day pressure to deliver, whereas the employing organisation may be somewhat more distant. We did not have a quantitive measure for this in all our cases and relied on qualitative data. In others we were able to construct a scale based on the extent to which clients' concerns were taken into account when making decisions.

Competing identities

These four identities exert conflicting pulls on the professional knowledge worker. Professionals have frequent and sometimes prolonged contact with their clients; their project team may have established its own identity; a strong organisational culture may give rise to an identity with their employer (Orlikowski, 2002); and a professional network outside the organisation may be a significant source of identity. Here identity is seen as emerging from complex, dynamic and reciprocal interactions between various stakeholders (Scott and Lane, 2000). The extent of the permeability of boundaries between firms and their clients (Hatch and Schultz, 2002; Swart *et al*, 2003) intensifies the extent to which various sources of identity can compete. These competing sources of identity are well recognised (Alvesson and Willmott, 2002; Albert and Whetten, 1985; Hatch and Schultz, 2002), and some attempts have been made to define the internal and external dimensions of organisational identity (Hatch and Schultz, 2002).

Perhaps the most likely is the tension between serving the interests of the client and serving the interests of the employing organisation (Alvesson, 2001). Employees are required as part of their job to pay close attention to the needs of their clients and to provide a high level of service, often forming close relationships with key members of their staff. However, they also have to take account of the objectives of their employing organisation – for example, to keep costs low, or to maximise opportunities for new business. These external ties that bring in critical resources may also enhance job mobility (Blyer and Coff, 2003; page 681).

Competing identities can also exist inside the knowledge-intensive firm. For example, the team identity (perhaps closely allied with a client identity) might be allowed to dominate in some firms so that all the efforts of the team members are focused on achieving their own goals, perhaps at the expense of wider organisational objectives. This may lead to the neglect of knowledge-sharing across the organisation.

There may also be a clash between adopting a professional focus and the wider interests of the organisation as a whole. Some employees may be looking to maximise their own development and their potential for development by being very selective about what work they take on, avoiding boring work and doing only work which interests them or strengthens their CV and market attractiveness. They may refuse to work for certain clients or at particular locations if they believe it will damage their own careers. The organisational identity of these employees may be so weak that they become poor corporate citizens, avoiding work – for example, administration and the line management of their staff – that they perceive to take time away from their own interests.

'Some employees may be looking to maximise ... their potential for development by being very selective about what work they take on ....'

These sources of competing identity represent different career routes for the professional. Within the software industry, the client may seek to recruit the highly competent IT professional from the software house with whom it has been working so closely. If the client identity is strong and the organisational identity is weak, then the employee may be inclined to pursue this. The close-knit team within the knowledge-intensive firm may tire of the constraints imposed by their employer and decide to set up their own business, perhaps taking some of the best clients with them. They may also avoid promotion to management positions. These and other career paths provide alternatives to those provided internally by the employing firm.

How, and how well, do firms manage such people in these circumstances? The problem is the need to ensure that the appropriation process is adequate, allowing for the capture of outputs generated from professionals' knowledge while avoiding excessive rent-sharing in the form of very high pay or 'golden handcuffs'. This involves the establishing of resource mobility barriers that are cost-effective. These must influence employee attitudes so that the 'inside' is more attractive than the 'outside', at least for a period long enough to solve the appropriation issue. To do this the firm has to find ways of managing or satisfying the professional's own identity needs.

Managing identities in two companies

We use two contrasting cases, both in the software industry, to explore the various identities as well as their impact on the careers of IT professionals (ITPs). The two companies we report on here are FinSoft and DataWare. Both are medium-sized software development firms and are primarily based in the south of England.

> FinSoft is engaged in the production of information systems solutions for around 20 clients who are mostly in the financial services sector. They employ around 400 people, principally on a single site. Most of their work was gained from a competitive tendering process or from projects with existing clients. However, more recently they have been acquiring business as the result of a strategic alliance with a large management consultancy. FinSoft was established around fifteen years ago and has grown very fast over the last five years. Traditionally, they have provided custom-built systems for individual clients. They are now, however, moving towards the production of a standard product which can then be modified to suit the needs of individual clients who can use their own employees to make changes if necessary. This shift is having widespread implications for the nature of the work, involving more product development and less bespoke work.

The first key finding in both our cases is that professional identity has a significant relationship with career satisfaction: the two are strongly and positively correlated.[2] In other words, professional knowledge workers who are satisfied with their careers also have a strong professional identity. It would therefore be critical for software organisations to seek to address their ITPs' need for professional identity if they are to resolve the development–retention dilemma. ITPs will remain with the organisation, and indeed contribute to the organisation, if their professional needs are met.

Secondly, there is a significant difference between the career satisfaction results in the two organisations (see Table 1). This enables us to see which of the organisations was more successful at managing its ITPs' careers, so we can draw some inferences regarding the management practices that address the dilemmas that we presented at the start of our report. Figures 6 and 7 (page 36) represent our findings diagrammatically.

> *'... professional knowledge workers who are satisfied with their careers also have a strong professional identity.'*

Professional identity

Employees in our two cases displayed quite divergent attitudes towards their jobs, and there was differing evidence for the existence of professional identity. ITPs in FinSoft enjoyed high levels of job autonomy and satisfaction, with influence over their work. Two-thirds of our

DataWare is a world leader in e-publishing services and Web delivery in the academic and professional sector. It has offices in the UK and the USA. The three core services that DataWare provide comprise: publisher services (online publishing platform), e-communities (creating content-rich vertical portals) and a search facility (deep Web content). Within these three core areas its mission is to be the dominant Web intermediary for professional and academic research. The vision that drives growth and financial success is the 'zero to 100 in 30', which translates into £0–£100 million financial growth within 30 months. The company wants to create a flourishing market and occupy a dominant position therein in the shortest possible time. The intensive growth that DataWare has undertaken has held various implications for how HR is practised in this knowledge-intensive business.

At director level the decision has been taken to integrate high technical standards with a more commercial approach, thereby combining both the services and product approaches to software development. This has led to the restructuring of the technical functions in the organisation along a project life-cycle approach: each project has set specifications (a product approach and managed by software engineers) and caters for bespoke client requests (a services approach managed by software developers). Within a project, software developers work with software engineers and information architects to deliver a high-quality service and product at the lowest possible cost to the organisation.

Table 1 | IT professionals' attitudes in FinSoft and DataWare

	FinSoft (n = 38)		DataWare (n = 25)	
	Mean	Standard deviation	Mean	Standard deviation
'My job is challenging.'	1.82	.80	2.48	.98
'The company attempts to make jobs interesting and varied.'	1.42	.50	1.68	.47
'I feel proud to tell people who I work for.'	1.79	.99	2.52	.75
'I feel loyal to my company.'	2.13	1.09	2.67	1.01
'I share the values of my company.'	2.11	9.50	2.93	.96
Organisational commitment	2.00	.82	2.70	.69
Sense of teamworking	2	1.12	2.74	1.24
Satisfaction with career opportunities	2.14	.94	3.10	1.07
Satisfaction with training	2.54	1.16	3.18	.76
Satisfaction with appraisal	2.32	.97	3.33	1.01
Satisfaction with information about company performance	2.45	.95	3.05	.80
Satisfaction with influence over decisions affecting job or work	2.83	.84	3.86	.73

FinSoft: alpha for organisational commitment 0.73
DataWare: alpha for organisational commitment 0.80
Scale: 1 – strongly agree/very satisfied/very strong;
           2 – agree/satisfied/strong;
           3 – neither agree nor disagree/neither satisfied nor dissatisfied/neither weak nor strong;
           4 – disagree/dissatisfied/weak;
           5 – strongly disagree/very dissatisfied/very weak

Figure 6 | Managing multiple identities in FinSoft

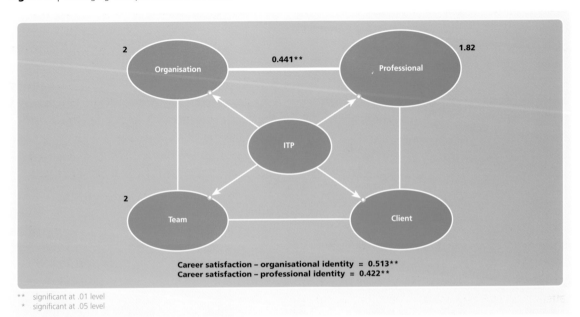

Figure 7 | Managing multiple identities in DataWare

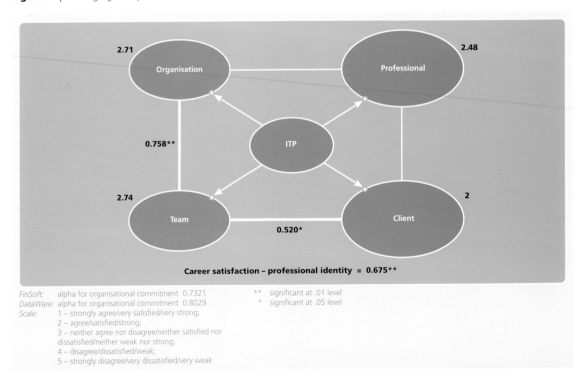

respondents felt they had a lot of influence over their jobs, and more than eight out of ten were either 'satisfied' or 'very satisfied' with the amount of influence they exercised. As one employee said:

I like the way we can organise the working day around what we want to do. You can manage your own time with no one looking over your shoulder.

You mostly have a free hand to make a success or failure of it – especially in a small team.

There is also clear evidence of the existence of a strong professional identity in FinSoft (see Table 1) shown by the responses to the statements[3] 'My job is challenging' (mean 1.82) and 'The company attempts to make the job as interesting and varied as possible' (mean 1.42). There is also a high level of satisfaction with career opportunities (mean 2.14). FinSoft is clearly able to serve the needs of its employees for autonomous, stimulating work, perhaps because of its emphasis on bespoke work for clients. As one participant indicated:

The people I work with are, on the whole, brilliant … and the work is quite challenging. There are plenty of opportunities … and the pay is good.

It's a good place to learn your trade, especially for graduates. It's a pleasant place to work, but if you are career-focused, you can still achieve things.

This situation contrasts with that at DataWare, where there were quite different employee attitudes. Only around a third of our respondents said they had a lot of influence over their jobs, and just over half were satisfied with that influence, and there were low levels of motivation. Professional identity was weaker in DataWare compared with FinSoft (see Table 1). Although there was reasonably good evidence that the company attempts to make jobs interesting and varied (mean 1.68), the big difference was on job challenge, where the mean score was 2.48 compared with 1.82 in FinSoft. One employee remarked:

At an engineering level I know how to engineer things – and despite recognising serious problems I get ignored. The work is not challenging or stimulating. I do not feel as if I have achieved anything.

This is perhaps reflected in the attitudes towards career development in this company, where the level of satisfaction with careers had a mean score of 3.10, compared with 2.14 in FinSoft. The ITPs in our two firms have different attitudes towards their jobs, and there is contrasting evidence for the existence of professional identity. FinSoft is able to satisfy the needs of its employees for autonomy, stretching work and career opportunities, and there is evidence of a strong professional identity. Employees in DataWare have much less influence over their jobs, lower satisfaction and much weaker professional identity.

We would expect knowledge-intensive firms such as these to be able to generate quite high levels of autonomy, satisfaction and professional identity because of the nature of the jobs. However, in the light of our examination of competing identities it seems that these firms may find it much more difficult to combine this with strong organisational and team identities. ITPs' strong professional identity may be at the expense of a strong organisational identity, or a good team spirit may weaken their commitment to the firm. But if a firm can manage these competing identities in such a way that it generates strong professional team and organisational identities, then it will have gone a long way towards solving the basic development–retention dilemma.

> **'… if a firm can [generate] strong professional team and organisational identities … it will have gone a long way towards solving the basic development–retention dilemma.'**

We now need to consider how able our two firms are to generate organisational commitment and team identity on the part of their ITPs.

Organisational, team and client identity

If we consider first the evidence of organisational identity, we find quite different attitudes on the part of our ITPs in our two companies. FinSoft stands out again as being able to generate high levels of commitment to the organisation on the part of its employees (see Table 1). In particular, its ITPs demonstrated high levels of pride (mean 1.79), loyalty (mean 2.13) and sharing company values (mean 2.11). Indeed, the combined measure

of organisational commitment was particularly high for FinSoft (mean 2.00). As one employee in FinSoft said:

It's a good place to work. People generally feel valued – you're not just another number and there's scope for advancement. They encourage you to make more of your skills and abilities.

This demonstrates quite clearly that it is possible to generate high levels of organisational commitment on the part of ITPs. The sense of teamworking was also strong in FinSoft (mean 2.00) although, according to qualitative data, identity with the client was somewhat weaker. One employee told us:

There is a sense of team responsibility – there's a no-blame culture, which is great. We all rally round to fix a problem before the customer sees it. We all get on socially, and we share the same values.

In contrast to FinSoft, DataWare demonstrates the problems involved with generating organisational commitment in this kind of organisation (see Table 1). ITPs in DataWare had much lower levels of pride (mean 2.52), loyalty (mean 2.67) and sharing values (mean 2.93), and their mean score for organisational commitment was 2.71. The sense of team spirit was in line with these responses (mean 2.74), although client identity was strong (mean 2.00). As one employee said:

We are all working on separate things. There is no team and no collaboration. Lots of work is done independently. There are low levels of team interaction. We are only a collection of individuals.

The key finding in FinSoft, therefore, is that it is possible to generate strong professional, team and organisational identities. More important still, we find that rather than competing, professional and organisational identity are associated with one another in FinSoft. More sophisticated analysis shows that our key measure of professional identity (job challenge) has a strong positive relationship with our measure of organisational commitment. There are also significant but weaker associations between job challenge and pride and loyalty. Team spirit is not, in FinSoft, associated with job challenge or any of the measures of organisational commitment. This may be because the team that an employee belongs to does not have a major impact on his or her experience of work, in that it is seen very much as part of the organisation as a whole rather than competing with it or an alternative to it. We were told by one employee:

There's no them and us, no bosses and workers, no confrontation. It's a big team.

This ability to combine professional identity and organisational commitment is associated with employees' satisfaction with their careers. Our analysis shows that satisfaction with careers is strongly associated with organisational commitment and with job challenge. We believe

that developing a strong commitment to FinSoft and providing opportunities for professional development are likely to satisfy ITPs' career needs and to make them less likely to leave the organisation.

There are lots of positives about FinSoft. It is still better than a lot of other companies. There is no reason to run – nowhere else is any better.

The key finding in DataWare is that there is no evidence of strong professional, organisational or team identities, although client identity is somewhat stronger. Indeed, it is likely that in this case these identities are competing. There is, for example, no association between job challenge and any of the measures of organisational commitment. DataWare has found it much more difficult to combine professional identity and commitment to the organisation. However, unlike FinSoft, there are strong associations between a sense of teamworking and loyalty to the organisation and a weaker association with pride. It seems that employee commitment in DataWare is much more strongly affected by employees' day-to-day experience of teamworking than in FinSoft, where the team the employee is in is less influential. There are also strong associations between team and client identity. These findings indicate a strong downward pull on the identities, effectively fragmenting the organisation.

Their satisfaction with careers is, however, associated with their professional identity in terms of job challenge and attempts to make the job interesting. It is also associated with loyalty, although we believe this is likely to be loyalty to the activity of the firm in terms of the support it provides to the research process, rather than loyalty to the firm itself.

Overall, then, FinSoft manages its ITPs in such a way that they are able to combine both professional and organisational identity, and both of these are associated with career satisfaction. The company is therefore able to develop its key human capital while simultaneously tying these employees in to the organisation. Its highly skilled professionals are more likely to invest their careers with FinSoft than elsewhere – for example, joining the client, setting up on their own or looking for a job through their professional networks.

DataWare, on the other hand, is unable to establish professional identity and have a scenario where the professional identity is competing with the organisational identity. This organisation is also not able to satisfy the professionals' knowledge needs, and most employees feel that they owe skill development and interesting work to their team and not to their organisation. These professionals are likely to direct their career attention away from the organisation and find jobs with their clients, establish smaller firms with their team members and use their external networks to find satisfying careers. DataWare will therefore lose its key human capital and will not be able to generate valuable intellectual capital.

In summary, this chapter set out to understand the various directions which a professional knowledge worker's career can take, and in particular to understand how these directions are influenced by the various identities that are shaped and managed in the organisation. Our key findings were these:

◘ Professional knowledge workers establish several forms of identity, owing to their particular employment context. These identities comprise their organisational identity (loyalty, pride and identification with organisational values), professional identity (the need for autonomy and job challenge within the organisation), team identity (the degree of team spirit and willingness to share knowledge within the team) and the client identity (the extent to which the employee identifies with the client's objectives, products, procedures and processes).

◘ Organisational, professional, team and client identities compete and can pull in opposite directions and begin to fragment the organisation.

◘ Each form of identity represents a possible career path for the professional knowledge worker.

◘ Our cases illustrated that there is a strong positive relationship between career satisfaction and professional identity. It is therefore important to pay attention to the development of professional identity when seeking to retain key talent in the organisation.

◘ In the case where employees were most satisfied with their careers, the organisation sought to manage the competing identities by developing both a strong organisational identity and a strong professional identity.

Our cases therefore demonstrate differing abilities to resolve the basic dilemma of meeting the needs of both individual ITPs and the companies that employ them. The key question now is: how can we explain this? How do our companies seek to manage these competing needs?

In the following chapter we explore the different ways in which our firms manage these conflicting needs, and we investigate how each identity is established and maintained. In some companies the result is that the employees' career needs are satisfied, whereas in others they are not. At the heart of the solution to competing identities is the ability to tie professional identity in with organisational identity ('My organisation develops my professional skills') and to ensure that neither client nor team identity overpowers the organisational identity. Our firms demonstrate quite different abilities to address this challenge and to erect barriers to the career mobility of their professional employees. Here we explore in detail the 'how to' of developing employees while ensuring that their skills and knowledge are retained.

Endnotes

1   These scales were combined as a result of factor analysis on a larger database, and we were able to retest the result for each of the companies reported here.

2   The correlations are 0.422 for FinSoft and 0.675 for DataWare. Details of the remaining correlations and their significance levels are not reported in the text but are available from the authors.

3   All statements were measured on a five-point Likert scale, 1 being high and 5 being low.

5 | HR practices for managing the careers of professional knowledge workers

This Briefing began by identifying the distinctive characteristics of professional knowledge workers and the types of firm in which they are employed. We then identified some knowledge-intensive situations which were critical to the success of these firms, and the dilemmas that had to be addressed when managing knowledge and managing professional knowledge workers. These tensions were then analysed using the concept of identity, particularly the notion of conflicting identities.

Here we turn our attention to the people management issues associated with this discussion. We do it in two ways.

- First, we draw on the wider research project and look at the people management practices that are particularly important for professional knowledge workers generally.

- We then turn our attention to look at these issues in more detail, drawing on our case studies.

HR practices for professionals

We can gain insights into the people management policies that are likely to influence the attitudes of professional knowledge workers by drawing on data from all 18 of the organisations we studied. This comprised a total of 769 respondents, of whom 270 were classified as professional employees. Our respondents were asked about a range of issues, including their attitudes towards their job and their employer, as well as their views on existing HR practices and their line manager, using a structured questionnaire.

Our focus is on the attitudes of professional workers in three key areas: their level of commitment to the organisation, their level of job satisfaction, and their motivation to work. We conducted sophisticated quantitative analysis to identify associations between these attitudes and a series of HR practices. Table 2 (overleaf) provides a summary of our analysis.

Table 2 | Associations between human resource policies and the attitudes of professional employees

HR policy/employee attitude	Organisational commitment	Job satisfaction	Employee motivation
Performance appraisal		+	+
Career opportunities	+	+	+
Teamworking			+
Work–life balance	+	+	
Rewards and recognition	+		
Involvement		+	
Relationship with line manager	+	+	
Job security			–
Effort	+		

+ positive association
– negative association
n = 769
Source: Bath survey of 18 companies (further details in Purcell *et al* (2003)

Perhaps the most important finding for our investigation is that the perception of career opportunities within the organisation is positively associated with employee commitment, job satisfaction and motivation. As we might expect, perceptions of the performance appraisal process are positively associated with job satisfaction and motivation, while perceptions of the relationship with line managers and of the work–life balance are positively associated with employee commitment and job satisfaction.

> '... people management policies most likely to have a positive effect on ... knowledge workers are those concerned with career opportunities, performance appraisal and the relationship with line managers.'

These findings are what might be anticipated for professional knowledge workers – for example, reward and recognition has a positive association only with employee commitment, and involvement is associated with motivation. Job security, on the other hand, is negatively associated with employee motivation.

In general terms the message here is that the people management policies most likely to have a positive effect on the attitudes of professional knowledge workers are those concerned with career opportunities, performance appraisal and the relationship with line managers. This finding develops the generic 'People and Performance' model we have discussed in more detail elsewhere (Purcell *et al*, 2003). It suggests that the people management policies that have the most important influence on employee attitudes will differ depending on the occupational group. The policies that improve job satisfaction, motivation and commitment for one group – professional knowledge workers in this instance – will not necessarily be the same as those for team leaders or shop-floor employees. This has potentially important implications for the homogeneity of organisational people management policies and is currently being investigated further. These findings also provide the broader context within which we can consider the more detailed case study examples.

HR practices for managing identities

Following the examination of our research relating to all professional knowledge workers, we now turn our attention to a more detailed examination of the people management practices that are key to managing the conflicting identities we discussed earlier. We will draw on our case studies to illustrate some of the practices that are particularly suited to managing each of these identities in turn.

Organisational identity

The practices aimed at managing organisational identity are essentially high-involvement practices which allow the employees to participate in the design and operation of people management policies in a variety of areas. They are designed to create a high degree of ownership of the culture and values of the organisation so that

they become embedded in the attitudes of the employees and the organisational routines.

Employee involvement in staffing policies is particularly important. In a number of our organisations employees are widely involved in making staffing decisions, not just in selection interviewing but in drawing up staffing policy.

The use of 'talent networks' is also well established, whereby existing formal and informal contacts are used to identify suitable employees rather than relying on third parties or advertising in the trade press. Employees were encouraged to retain their links with their former universities as well as with colleagues at previous employers. These informal networks allowed the discussion of possible vacancies and employees who might be suitable to fill them. Employees effectively became the eyes and ears of the recruitment process.

As one respondent put it:

We know people with hot skills in the industry through university friends and by just meeting in the pub on Fridays with other techies.

This process was more formalised in some organisations – for example, in Chemlab, as shown in Figure 8 (overleaf). Here, staff were recruited straight from university, possibly following a period of industrial placement which was in effect an extended interview. Their recruitment as chemists with a PhD provided them with a form of apprenticeship which made them very aware of the need to work in networks both within and outside the organisation.

Figure 8 | Chemlab network

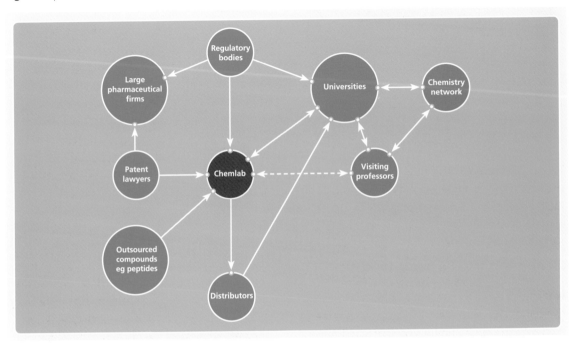

In FinSoft there was a strong emphasis on recruitment practices aimed at developing an internal labour market and maintaining the organisational identity. There was a clear policy of recruiting non-technical graduates directly from university, and selection criteria stressed the fit with the existing organisational values. However, recently some more experienced managers had been recruited to fill the role of project managers because there was insufficient talent internally, and this had posed some threat to the organisational values.

Selection methods often pay very careful attention to the extent of cultural and organisational fit. Often these firms are not only looking at technical skills, which in some senses are relatively easy to spot because they can be assessed and are formally certificated, but are also searching for non-technical skills. These might include how well applicants can communicate their ideas and how able and willing they are to share their knowledge.

In Bespoke Ware technical ability is not considered the most important element and the culture of the organisation drives the recruitment process. As a senior software engineer who shared responsibility for recruitment remarked: 'I think of it as inviting someone to a party. You know, sometimes you invite people who you want to come along – not necessarily those who deserve to come along.

The successful organisations also seek to establish their own internal knowledge networks as part of their graduate development programme. As we will discuss, this helped to bring the professional and organisational identity together and to develop organisationally specific knowledge that was less transferable to competitors. It was associated with a strong emphasis on the companies' growing their own employees rather than bringing large numbers of people in from outside.

These knowledge networks were also part of a more widespread communications policy. For example, in FinSoft they developed formal communications mechanisms based on what they referred to as 'T groups', which were non-hierarchical, non-specialist groupings whose task was to communicate upwards and downwards. This was in addition to the more formal mechanisms such as an annual company-wide meeting and lunchtime meetings on more technical subjects.

Professional identity

Perhaps the most explicit way of providing opportunities for professional development is seen in the type of work that the organisation undertakes. Other strategies include skills development through project management and attention to vocational needs. The nature of the measures in the performance management system and the type of reward and recognition received also had a great impact on the development of professional identity.

We now discuss each of these sets of practices.

Some of our organisations paid attention to the development of unique skills and therefore chose to take on only bespoke contracts that were likely to provide interesting and stimulating work for their employees. For example, FinSoft traditionally concentrated on bespoke software but has recently been adding products to its portfolio of activities. This emphasis on customised work for clients is likely to make it much easier to provide challenging and interesting work for its employees. Employees are often presented with poorly defined client problems that require novel solutions. This orientation is reflected in their relatively sophisticated multiple-team-based internal structures, with a mix of traditional functional departments and more non-traditional structures which place an emphasis on sharing knowledge and best practice.

DataWare, on the other hand, concentrates on providing relatively standardised products and services which present less of a challenge to ITPs. In fact, because of its fast growth the company has divided its software work into software engineering and software design. Consequently, its software engineers 'build' relatively standard products that are then tailored by software designers to the needs of specific clients. This also means that there is a series of large project teams that often have specialist sub-groups within them. There is a committee structure at senior levels, but below this there are more traditional functional departments.

> **'Some of our organisations sought to ensure that their employees took ownership of their own development.'**

Linked to the opportunities to develop cutting-edge skills were the firms' developmental philosophies. Some of our organisations sought to ensure that their employees took ownership of their own development. They stressed the need for knowledge-sharing within and between project teams, effectively establishing communities of practice. For example, the vocational teams in FinSoft brought together employees doing the same task on different client project teams to discuss issues of common interest. In other firms the project structure was key to developing knowledge, as evident in Bespoke Ware.

In summary, the key characteristics of the developmental approach that built a professional identity were:

In Bespoke Ware the most competent person was selected to be project manager – who might not always be the most senior person on the team. This allowed those staff who wanted a chance to develop their project management skills to do so, and gave people an opportunity to move between roles. One respondent told us: 'We don't just have people who do only project management – and quite honestly, with the type of work we do you will never find someone who will want to do only project management work: it would be far too boring and we want to keep our skills at the cutting edge.' This policy was complemented by a fluid project structure through which staff were encouraged to move between project teams to maintain a level of interesting work and to broaden their skill range.

- ◘ the development of cutting-edge skills through interesting, bespoke work

- ◘ informal learning from one another, leading to the development of knowledge-sharing abilities

- ◘ skill development through work design in the project team

- ◘ some formal learning that complements the culture of learning established by the professionals in the organisation

- ◘ freedom to learn from professional networks provided by the organisation.

One of the most important areas for professional knowledge workers is their involvement in the development of performance management systems. These employees are often very sensitive about these systems because, as we have outlined, they feel a high degree of ownership over their skills and knowledge, and take great pride in achieving advanced standards of performance.

Moreover, knowledge-intensive outcomes tend to be ambiguous and often difficult to measure. We found that because the outcomes were so ambiguous, knowledge workers themselves frequently took over the development and implementation of performance managing systems, in this way often generating a strong sense of ownership over the process. Some firms made their commitment tangible by allowing staff to dedicate some of their chargeable time to performance management activities.

The forms of recognition are also very important. As we saw when looking at the results generally, these types of employee are not so much concerned with financial reward as with various non-financial rewards. For example, the reward of redundant time or of the opportunity to attend a training course or a conference might well be highly valued.

A number of these employees were also concerned about achieving a suitable work–life balance:

It's pretty amazing how much they care for the people who work for them. Others can't believe how well FinSoft does it. There is a good understanding that people have commitments outside work.

> **'Most successful organisations had fluid project teams with relatively permeable boundaries.'**

Team identity

Many professional knowledge employees spend much of their working time in their team. In fact, for some their primary experience of the organisation is through the team. We have seen that this can have a fragmenting effect on organisational structure and weaken organisational identity. People management practices towards teamworking are therefore vital to managing the competing identities.

Most successful organisations had fluid project teams with relatively permeable boundaries. Employees found it easy to move in and out of teams and to engage in cross-boundary working. This might involve a formal policy of staff rotation to avoid teams becoming too fixed and fragmenting the organisation, perhaps allied to more informal encouragement to move across boundaries.

FinSoft has a mixture of client and product teams, some of which are hierarchical, the larger ones having technical sub-groups. Membership of these teams is fluid: employees join and leave depending on the stage in the project cycle. Project team boundaries are permeable because of this staff movement and because of the vocational and communications teams we described earlier.

In DataWare there are a small number of large product and client teams that have developed quite an elaborate hierarchy. The emphasis on technical specialism means that there are limited opportunities for movement between the teams. Not only are boundaries between the teams strong, but in the larger teams the emphasis on specialist functional areas limits the opportunities for sharing information and knowledge – a process that is made even more difficult when members of project teams are based in different countries.

On some occasions opportunities for professional development could be created through the use of sub-projects – small pieces of work carried out on a temporary basis in response to a client's request. These were often set up to teach new employees organisation-specific skills and to introduce them to key clients in the organisation. Sub-projects could also be used as an effective means of integrating existing skills into new product designs and giving employees the opportunity to use current knowledge in the application of new market developments.

A number of our companies invested heavily in the development of social capital. This not only included the normal kind of sponsorship of social activities, such as sports activities, but also more elaborate and embedded forms – for example, those in FinSoft, where a part-time member of

staff was appointed as a 'Visionaire' whose task was to get staff to participate in outside-work activities. These activities were designed to allow employees to cross boundaries and to encourage staff to meet and share knowledge informally. In Bespoke Ware the simple act of meeting together in the pub at Friday lunchtime provided an informal knowledge network.

This approach towards teamworking often reflected a wider approach towards organisational structure. For example, the most successful firms developed structures that sought to avoid high degrees of fragmentation caused by hierarchy and specialisation in favour of a more fluid approach, as seen in Bespoke Ware. Here there was no specialist HR department, but instead people management policy and process issues were shared out to a series of committees who took responsibility for particular areas – for example, performance management.

Client identity

For many years consultants and experts have been exhorting professional service firms to adopt a client focus. However, as we have seen, there are dangers involved because of the potential for fragmenting the organisation and weakening organisational identity. The problem is that these firms may become organised solely along client lines, with few opportunities for knowledge-sharing, and with individual power based on the size of the contracts that the person is managing. The situation can be made worse if the client insists that 'their team' maintains high levels of confidentiality. This in turn can weaken organisational identity, which then has implications for career satisfaction and labour turnover, as seen (for example) in DataWare.

There are clearly very strong pressures to satisfy the client, especially where the firm is small and vulnerable to the whims of the client. Strong potential exists here for the client to dictate everything, including, crucially, the allocation of staff. Our successful firms sought to be client-focused rather than client-driven. They paid close attention to the needs of their clients, but they would not allow the clients to interfere in ways that were detrimental in the long and medium term to the interests of their employees and of the firm. This involved taking brave decisions in the face of client pressure.

The importance of the client is also seen in the premium placed on client relationship management skills. These involve not only preparing a bid for new business but also managing the contract once it has been awarded. Successful companies explicitly recognise the importance of these skills and shape their recruitment, selection and development programmes in ways aimed at growing these skills internally.

The allocation of resources to new projects was very sensitive for the client, the organisation and the employee. The client would often be sold a project on the basis of team membership.

However, managers in the organisations were seeking to balance the concerns of the client, of the employing firm and of the employee. They had to consider what was good for the client, what was good for the development of the employee, and what was good for the success of the firm.

This might involve balancing a request by a client that names an employee as vital to the project and the request perhaps by the same employee not to remain on that job any longer because it is boring and involves staying away from home a long time. If this situation cannot be resolved to the satisfaction of the employee, he or she may feel powerful enough to threaten to leave, and possibly threaten also to take the client with him or her.

> In FinSoft it is the director of Human Capital rather than the operations director who controls the allocation of staff to projects. This is seen as essential to maintain a balance between providing employees with interesting work and opportunities for development on the one hand, and servicing the needs of the client on the other.

One way of restricting the power of the client is to ensure that a balance is struck between the development of client and market capital.

> *'[Managers] had to consider what was good for the client, ... for the development of the employee, and what was good for the success of the firm.'*

Client capital involves the expertise and knowledge about that client, its products and the sector in which it operates – this is often a way of gaining a good reputation and doing high-value work.

Market capital involves the development of skills and knowledge that are more generally useful within the market. It might be developed by carrying out research, and making presentations as a way of furthering knowledge, keeping people and possibly gaining business. However, collecting this kind of more general capital can be expensive, and there may be no immediate payoff. Nonetheless, a number of our firms saw it as a key aspect of their networking activities and invested heavily in this kind of market capital accumulation.

More generally, some of our companies redefined some of the tensions that we identified. For example, rather than seeing a tension between managing clients and managing employees, they argued that these relationship skills were essentially similar. In Finsoft, for instance, one key theme is the recognition that the skills needed for managing relations with employees are very similar to those needed for managing relations with clients – which was reflected in FinSoft's aim to be 'the best company in the world to work for and the best company in the world to work with.' In 2002 FinSoft came fifth in the UK Sunday Times Top 100 Firms to Work For list.

> '[For our successful firms'] business strategy was aimed at establishing a virtuous circle that combined the needs of the organisation and of individual knowledge workers.'

Implications for policy and practice

We began this chapter by drawing on the wider research project to highlight the people management policies associated with improvements in the job satisfaction, motivation and commitment of professional knowledge workers in general. We noted that policies concerned with career opportunities, performance appraisal and the relationship with line managers were most likely to have a positive effect on the attitudes of these employees. We then looked in more detail at our companies, concentrating on the way they sought to manage the conflicting sources of identity that their professional knowledge workers experience. Not all of our companies were equally successful at this – which has a number of implications for policy and practice.

The key issue appears to be the extent to which these conflicting identities were managed in a way that was appropriate to the organisation. For example, FinSoft was successful because it used its people management practices to encourage organisational and professional identity and to ensure that the client identity did not dominate. This fitted the business strategy of paying close attention to the needs of both the client and the organisation. Other organisations, such as DataWare, did not have such a coherent policy, allowing the team and client much greater importance, with negative consequences for their ability to create and share knowledge internally.

Our successful firms used a combination of business strategy and people management practices in an attempt to deal with the conflicting needs of managing knowledge and managing knowledge workers. Their business strategy was aimed at establishing a virtuous circle that combined the needs of the organisation and of individual knowledge workers. If a firm possessed intellectual capital that was rare and difficult to copy, its chances of gaining high-value contracts which involved interesting work were increased. These types of contract in turn made it more likely that the company would be able to retain its most valuable employees, whose presence gave it a better chance of winning the high-value work it sought. A break in this virtuous circle could lead to a reduced ability to compete successfully for high-value work, making it more difficult for a firm to retain its valued employees.

Although the use of people management policies varied between our companies, a number of such policies were common:

◘ the involvement of professional knowledge workers in the establishment of people management practices – this ensures that practices are embedded, and links other forms of identity with the organisational identity

◘ recruitment and selection practices that were facilitated by internal and external networks and culturally driven

◘ training and development aimed at creating organisationally specific knowledge both within and between project teams

◘ reward and recognition that took the form of financial and non-financial incentives

◘ performance management systems that demonstrated the involvement of high-level professional knowledge workers in both their design and implementation

◘ the development of social capital perceived as an important means of facilitating interaction and knowledge-sharing

◘ attempts being made to acquire both client and market capital.

However, as we have argued elsewhere (Purcell *et al*, 2003), simply possessing these policies is no guarantee of success, because many of them can be easily purchased from a consultant or copied from a textbook. In the organisations we studied it is the processes and routines used by line managers and team leaders to bring these policies to life that really affects the day-to-day experiences of employees. Indeed, the generation of this 'organisational process advantage', as it has been referred to (Boxall and Purcell, 2003), is likely to be especially important in these firms. The reliance solely on formal policies and specialised departments is particularly inappropriate.

Many of our companies simply did not have specialist HR departments, either because they were not of sufficient size or because they choose not to organise themselves in this way. This did not mean that these people management activities were necessarily neglected. Far from it. In some companies the absence of a formal department was a positive sign, because it illustrated that people management responsibilities were effectively distributed throughout the organisation. Line managers were actively engaged not just in the delivery of these policies but also, crucially, in their design. The policies and the philosophies which underlay them and the procedures which accompanied them were firmly embedded in the organisational routines and ways of working. Consequently, there was a much higher degree of ownership over these policies and practices than when they were owned by a specialist department.

This high level of ownership increased the chances of resolving the tension between managing knowledge and managing knowledge workers. Indeed, our successful companies recognised that there could be a synergy between managing knowledge and managing knowledge workers rather than a tension. Their people management processes and their processes for knowledge-sharing were carefully matched, mutually reinforcing and pervasive. These firms became more skilled at meeting both their own knowledge needs and those of their professional employees. This enabled the conversion of human capital into tangible intellectual capital, which provided the foundation for sustainable competitive advantage.

Appendix | Case study organisations

Bespoke Ware

Bespoke Ware is a small software house based on two sites in the south-west of England. It was founded in 1986 by three software engineers who wanted to focus on the development of bespoke software in embedded systems. At the time of the research Bespoke Ware employed 46 people, of whom 30 were software engineers, and it had a turnover of £2 million. Bespoke Ware's advantage in the marketplace is based on its dominant position in a niche market. Its main competitors are individual contractors.

Chemlab

Chemlab is a leading manufacturer and supplier of chemicals for life-science research. The firm was formed by the merger, in 1994 of two companies that had originated in university research departments. Since the merger, the company has grown rapidly, the core activity being the chemical synthesis of complex organic molecules, particularly those exhibiting biological activity. Chemlab employs 60 people engaged in the production of catalogue compounds, custom synthesis and contract research services. Turnover in 2002–2003 was £5 million, with operating profits of £1 million.

FinSoft

FinSoft provides software products and services for around 20 clients in the financial services sector. It was established in 1986 and at the time of the research employed around 400 people on one principal site in the UK and smaller sites abroad. In 2001 it had a turnover of £20 million. FinSoft's reputation in the industry is derived from its ability to solve the complex problems of linking legacy systems using highly customised solutions. It has more recently developed a standardised product to solve these problems which can then be developed by clients.

DataWare

DataWare is a world leader in e-publishing services and Web delivery in the academic and professional sector. It has offices in the UK and abroad, and at the time of the research employed around 200 people. The three core services that DataWare provide comprise publisher services (online publishing platform), e-communities (creating content-rich vertical portals) and a search facility (deep Web content). Turnover in 2001–2002 was £4.3 million.

References

ALBERT, S. and WHETTEN, D. A. (1985)

'Organizational identity', in L. L. Cummings and B. M. Staw (eds), *Research in Organizational Behavior* (Vol. 7). Greenwich, CT, JAI Press

ALVESSON, M. (1995)

The Management of Knowledge Intensive Companies. Berlin/New York, de Gruyter

ALVESSON, M. (2001)

'Social identity and the problem of loyalty in knowledge intensive companies', *Journal of Management Studies*, 37 (8), 1101–23

ALVESSON, M. and WILLMOTT, H. (2002)

'Identity regulation as organizational control: producing the appropriate individual', *Journal of Management Studies*, 39 (5), 619–44

ARTHUR, M. B. and ROUSSEAU, D. M. (1996)

'The boundaryless career as a new employment principle', in M. B. Arthur and D. M. Rousseau (eds) *The Boundaryless Career: A new employment principle for a new organizational era.* Oxford, OUP

ASHFORTH, B. E. and MAEL, F. (1989)

'Social identity theory and the organization', *Academy of Management Review*, 14 (1), 20–39

BLYER, M. and COFF, R. W. (2003)

'Dynamic capabilities: social capital, and rent appropriation – ties that split pies', *Strategic Management Journal*, 24, 677–86

BAUMARD, P. (1999)

Tacit Knowledge in Organisations. London, Sage

BONTIS, N. (1998)

'Intellectual capital: an exploratory study that develops measures and models', *Management Decision*, 36 (2), 63–76

BOWMAN, C. and SWART, J.

(under review) 'The role of embedded capital in the capture of value', *Journal of Management Studies*

BROWN, A. D. and STARKEY, K. (2000)

'Organizational identity and learning: a psychodynamic perspective', *Academy of Management Review*, 25 (1), 102–20

BROWN, M. E. (1969)

'Identification and some conditions of organizational involvement', *Administrative Science Quarterly*, 14, 346–55

CAPPELLI, P. (ed.) (1999)

The New Deal at Work: Managing the market-driven workforce. Boston, Harvard Business School Press

HATCH, M. J. and SCHULTZ, M. (2002)

'The dynamics of organizational identity', *Human Relations*, 55 (8), 989–1017

LABOUR FORCE SURVEY, 2000

Available online at www.dfes.goc.uk/statistics

LEONARD-BARTON, D. (1995)

Wellsprings of Knowledge. Boston, Harvard Business School Press

MARCH, J. G. (1991)

'Exploration and exploitation in organizational learning', *Organization Science*, 2, 71–87

MORRIS, T (2000)

'Promotion policies and knowledge bases in the professional service firm', in M. Peiperl, M. Arthur, R. Goffee and T. Morris (eds) *Career Frontiers: New conceptions of working lives.* Oxford, OUP

MUELLER, F. (1996)

'Human resources as strategic assets: an evolutionary resource-based theory', *Journal of Management Studies*, 33 (6), 757–85

NELSON, R. and WINTER, S. G. (1982)

An Evolutionary Theory of Economic Change. Cambridge, Mass, Harvard University Press

NONAKA, I. (1994)

'A dynamic theory of organizational knowledge creation', *Organization Science*, 5 (1), 14–35

NONAKA, I. and TAKEUCHI, H. (1995)

The Knowledge-Creating Company. Oxford, OUP

ORLIKOWSKI, W. J. (2002)

'Knowing in practice: enacting a collective capability in distributed organizing', *Organization Science*, 13 (3), 249–73

POLANYI, M. (1966)

The Tacit Dimension. London, Routledge & Kegan Paul

PURCELL, J., KINNIE, N., HUTCHINSON, S. *et al* (2003)

Understanding the People and Performance Link: Unlocking the black box. London, CIPD

SCOTT, S. and LANE, V. (2000)

'A stakeholder approach to organizational identity', *Academy of Management Review*, 25 (1), 43–63

SEELY BROWN, J. (2002)

'Research that reinvents the corporation', *Harvard Business Review*, August, 105–15

SWART, J. and KINNIE, N. (2003)

'Knowledge intensive firms: the influence of the client on HR systems', *Human Resource Management Journal*, 13 (3), 37–55

SWART, J., KINNIE, N. and PURCELL, J. (2003)

People and Performance in Knowledge Intensive Firms. London, CIPD

TAJFEL, H. and TURNER, J. C. (1985)

'The social identity theory of intergroup behaviour', in S. Worchel and W. G. Austin (eds) *The Psychology of Intergroup Relations* (2nd edn.). Chicago, Nelson-Hall

VALCOUR, P. M. and SNELL, S. A. (2002)

'The boundaryless career and work force flexibility: developing human and social capital for organisational and individual advantage'. Paper presented at the 2002 Annual Meeting of the Academy of Management, Denver, CO.

VON GLINOW, M. A. (1988)

New Professionals: Managing today's high-technology employees. London, Harper Business